CATS SET IV

CALICO CATS

Nancy Furstinger
ABDO Publishing Company

Lions, Tigers, and Cats

Domestic cats can trace their ancestry back to African wildcats. Ancient Egyptians tamed these animals around 3,500 years ago. The cats kept rats and mice out of granaries where the harvests were stored. Egyptians believed cats were sacred.

This cheetah stalks its prey at sunrise in Kenya.

Cats continue to be treasured as pets. Today, there are more than 40 different **breeds** of **domestic** cats. Both big and small cats belong to the **Felidae** family. This family contains 38 species, including cheetahs, jaguars, lions, and tigers.

Even though they are tame, house cats act a lot like their larger cousins. All cats are natural hunters. They have superior senses of sight, smell, and hearing. But, big cats cannot purr and small cats cannot roar.

Some domestic cats can have spots similar to the markings on this jaguar. This wildcat is found in South America.

5

CALICO CATS

Calico is the American name for a **tortoiseshell** and white cat. Calico cats most likely originated in Asia. There, these cats were considered lucky charms. They were revered for the rarity of their curious coloring.

Male calicoes are even more unusual. This is because most calicoes are female. The gene that causes the calico's distinct coloring is **sex-linked**. Only about one in 3,000 calico cats is male. And, a male calico is usually **sterile**.

There are many myths and legends about calico cats. In Japan, tricolored cats were thought to have magical powers. In England, people believed that anyone who played with calico kittens would be able to see the future.

Calico cats are not registered with the **Cat Fanciers' Association (CFA)**. This is because they are not an actual **breed**. However, the CFA acknowledges 16 different breeds that can have the calico pattern.

Patches of cream or white are desirable on a calico cat's face. This coloring helps bring out the eyes, which are usually a darker color.

QUALITIES

Today, calico cats are still considered lucky by people who share their homes with them. These adorable cats capture hearts wherever they go.

Besides its coloring, there are not many qualities specific to the calico. Its personality often depends on the **breed**.

Most cats are very independent. But if properly cared for and **socialized**, your calico should be friendly and affectionate. Cats usually have calm, charming natures. And most cats enjoy companions, such as cats, dogs, or children.

Opposite page: Cats are natural hunters and love to spend time outside. They will perch any place they can find that is high above the action.

COAT AND COLOR

All calico cats have a tricolored coat. Most are white with splotches of orange and black. Some calicoes have coats of white, cream, and gray. These are called dilute calicoes.

The calico's coat can be long or short, depending on the **breed**. A patch of white often decorates the **muzzle**. And, white socks stretch up the legs.

A calico's colors should appear in distinct patches. And, the same percentage of each color usually covers the body.

In 2001, the calico became the official cat of Maryland. Calicoes share splashes of orange, black, and white with the Baltimore oriole, Maryland's state bird. The Baltimore checkerspot butterfly, Maryland's state insect, also has these colors!

Like snowflakes, no two calico cats ever have the same pattern!

SIZE

Cats are powerfully built animals. They are designed to be hunters. They usually land on their feet if they are dropped. When a cat is frightened, it arches its back and bristles its coat in order to look larger.

It is always a good idea to have an identification collar for your cat. Especially if it plays outdoors!

Calicoes come in various sizes, depending on the **breed**. Most cats weigh between 6 and 10 pounds (3 and 5 kg). Some cats can weigh as much as 28 pounds (13 kg)! Female cats are usually smaller than males.

12

Calicoes can have green, gold, yellow,
hazel, or blue eyes.

CARE

Cats use their rough tongue to clean their coat. Because of this, they can swallow a lot of hair. So, they need human help with grooming. Regular brushing prevents hair balls from forming in their stomach.

Cats need to be entertained. Toys such as a ball or catnip mouse keep them busy for hours. An indoor climbing tree lets them perch above the action. And, a scratching post allows them to sharpen their claws without damaging furniture.

Like all cats, calicoes can be trained to use a **litter box**. Cats have a natural instinct to bury their waste. Place the litter box in a spot away from your cat's feeding bowls. And remember to clean the box daily!

Your calico will need to visit the veterinarian for a yearly checkup and **vaccines**. The veterinarian can **spay** or **neuter** your pet as well.

This dilute calico is having its yearly checkup.

FEEDING

When you adopt your calico, ask what type of cat food it was served. Keep feeding your cat this familiar food. If you want to change food, slowly mix in a new brand. This will prevent your cat from getting an upset stomach.

Cats are natural meat eaters. So, they need balanced diets that include protein, such as fish, poultry, or beef. Commercial cat food can provide your calico with all the **nutrients** it needs.

The three kinds of commercial cat food are dry, semimoist, and canned. Read the label for advice on how much to feed your cat based on its age, weight, and health. Serve the food, as well as fresh, clean water, in stainless steel bowls.

In addition to a healthy diet, your calico also needs a warm bed in a quiet spot. During the day, cats can sleep up to 16 hours! They are more active at night.

Cats will sleep just about anywhere. This lazy calico has made itself comfortable in a flower bed.

KITTENS

All kittens are born blind and deaf. After about three to five weeks, they can eat soft food and wrestle with other kittens. By the time they are 12 weeks old, the kittens can join their new human families.

Calico kittens pop up in **litters** of many different **breeds**. It's impossible to plan a litter consisting completely of calicoes. Getting the correct coat coloring is like a game of chance.

The calico markings on this kitten are already clearly defined.

Kittens love milk. But sometimes, older cats are unable to digest it.

BUYING A KITTEN

Cats can live for 15 to 20 years. So, adopting one is a big commitment. If you are thinking of adopting a calico kitten or cat, there are many **breeds** to choose from. Among these are the Maine coon, the Persian, the Manx, and the Scottish fold.

Choose a smart, sassy kitten. The kitten should glow with good health. It should have glossy fur, bright eyes, and clean ears and nose. A curious, playful kitten who prances over to play might be the one to adopt!

A calico Maine coon

20

Breeders, rescue shelters, and veterinary clinics are
all places to search for a calico cat or kitten.

GLOSSARY

breed - a group of animals sharing the same appearance and characteristics. A breeder is a person who raises animals. Raising animals is often called breeding them.

Cat Fanciers' Association (CFA) - a group that sets the standards for judging all breeds of cats.

domestic - animals that are tame.

Felidae - the scientific Latin name for the cat family.

litter - all of the kittens born at one time to a mother cat.

litter box - a box filled with cat litter, which is similar to sand. Cats use litter boxes to dispose of their waste.

muzzle - an animal's nose and jaws.

neuter (NOO-tuhr) - to remove a male animal's reproductive organs.

nutrient - a substance found in food and used in the body to promote growth, maintenance, and repair.

sex-linked - controlled or affected by a gene that determines the sex of an animal or human.

socialize - to accustom an animal or a person to spending time with others.

spay - to remove a female animal's reproductive organs.

sterile - unable to produce offspring.

tortoiseshell - a color pattern of the domestic cat that consists of patches of black, red, and cream.

vaccine (vak-SEEN) - a shot given to animals or humans to prevent them from getting an illness or disease.

WEB SITES

To learn more about calico cats, visit ABDO Publishing Company on the World Wide Web at **www.abdopub.com**. Web sites about these cats are featured on our Book Links page. These links are routinely monitored and updated to provide the most current information available.

INDEX

A

adoption 16, 18, 20
Africa 4
Asia 6

C

care 14, 15, 16, 17
Cat Fanciers'
    Association 7
character 8, 20
coat 10, 12, 14, 20
color 6, 7, 8, 10,
    11, 18

E

ears 5, 18, 20
Egypt 4
England 6
eyes 5, 18, 20

F

Felidae 5
food 14, 16, 18

G

grooming 14

H

health 16, 20
history 4, 5, 6
hunting 4, 5, 12

J

Japan 6

K

kittens 6, 18, 20

L

legs 10
life span 20
litter box 14

M

Maryland 11
muzzle 10

N

neuter 15
nose 5, 20

P

play 14, 18, 20

S

scratching post 14
senses 5, 18
sex-linked gene 6
size 12
sleep 17
spay 15

V

veterinarian 15

W

water 16
wildcat 4, 5